Belief and Unbelief

Peppercanister Books

Distributed in Ireland by
The Dedalus Press,
13 Moyclare Road, Baldoyle, Dublin 13

in the United Kingdom by
Carcanet Press Limited,
28-34 Cross Street, Manchester M2 7AQ

in North America by
Syracuse University Press, Inc., 621 Skytop Road,
Suite 110, Syracuse, New York 13244

First published 2007

© Thomas Kinsella 2007. All rights reserved.

The Dedalus Press
ISBN 978 1 904556 74 9
www.dedaluspress.com

Carcanet Press Ltd.
ISBN 978 1 85754 974 4
www.carcanet.co.uk

Printed in Ireland by Betaprint Ltd., Dublin

Cover image: Opus Sectile della Basilica di Giunio Basso,
Roma, Musei Capitolini,
Courtesy Archivio Fotografico dei Musei Capitolini

The Dedalus Press receives financial support from
The Arts Council, An Chomhairle Ealaíon, Ireland

Thomas Kinsella

Belief and Unbelief

Peppercanister 27

ACKNOWLEDGEMENTS

'Superfresh' and 'Legendary Figures, in Old Age' first appeared in *PN Review* and subsequently, together with 'Echo' and 'Addendum', in *Wingspan: A Dedalus Sampler* (ed. Pat Boran), Dedalus Press, 2006.

Contents

Novice	7
Delirium	9
Superfresh	11
A Morsel of Choice	12
Echo	13
Art Object	14

Belief and Unbelief

Legendary Figures, in Old Age	17
Lost Cause	18
Ceremony	19
Foetus of Saint Augustine	20
Genesis	21
Prayer I	22
Prayer II	23
Addendum	24

Novice

I was out late, by myself,
in the last light near the river
    —beginning to be solitary in my habits.

When a pale small ghost body
landed on a stone near my foot. Fragile
    at a short distance, with delicate wings,

but hard and alien up close:
the four white narrow wings
    open down distinct and flat;

the jointed gut pointed back straight;
the little stick legs angled
    up off the back and forward off the neck;

the black bead eyes staring nowhere;
the pipe mouth coiled back small and tight.
    Exactly the same as in the animal book

in the old wardrobe in the back bedroom,
with the big grey pictures:
    the species that sucks and swallows

only while it is growing; that cannot eat
once it reaches maturity.
    Designed for its exact needs.

*

My senses alive in the night:
the sounds of the river flowing broad in the shadows
    past the end of the field.

I could smell the old clothes covering the animal book
—with my own name on the first page, written
    beside a date from years before I was born;

and a dry ancient smell off the death moth
—my foot squeezing it and its little glands
    into the moss on the stone.

Delirium

I

Uproar ended.
Arms and elbows
strapped to the torso.
Pelvis straining
up from the table.

Joints still jerking;
wired to a window
high in the wall:
the distant healer
and his masked assistants.

Veins still beating
thick in the temples.
Will drained bare
back to the dark
and the depth that I came from.

II

The doctor halted
at the foot of the bed
in his hospital coat.

In his late twenties.
Recently qualified,
to my dazed respect.

Our eyes
feeding on each other.

III

Someone will please get me
out of this place

away from the familiars
nosing around the screen

and passing at the slack gap of my feet,
saying nothing.

Come to see us sick
that would not see us well.

Superfresh

I pulled the trolley to one side,
into the recess with the special bread,
to find the list in one of my pockets
and check the next choices.
The leather overcoat wet and heavy,
my collar raw against my beard from the snow.

A woman stopped in front of me. Her face thin,
her voice sharp.
                 In what have I offended ...?

But she was asking, in a thick accent,
where I came from; saying
that she came from Russia.
She stood there, no longer young,
waiting for an answer.

                         I understood;
and told her where I came from.
Her eyes faded. She spoke again,
her voice distant, saying something
nondescript and lonely. Our spirits
disengaged, somewhere above the Alps.

In my leather overcoat; in from the Winter;
bearded; not from Russia;
I touched the backs of my fingers

against her cheek, abstract-intimate,
in a fragrance off the shelves
of Italian loaves and French boule.

A Morsel of Choice

She was chatting among the crowd at the church porch,
smiling with her toothy horse-face,
her eyes active like damp meat
behind her large spectacles, watching everywhere.

I pictured my thumb and forefinger
plucking something wet off her tongue,
and caught a distant taste of the raw random

that walks at the side of Man,
to unsettle his wandering purpose
and unfocus his old age.

Echo

He cleared the thorns
from the broken gate,
and held her hand
through the heart of the wood
to the holy well.

They revealed their names
and told their tales
as they said that they would
on that distant day
when their love began.

And hand in hand
they turned to leave.
When she stopped and whispered
a final secret
down to the water.

Art Object

Her face buried in the live neck,
her top lip pulled back,
the fangs dug deep.

She is aware of nothing
but the immediate need.
Her young prey is aware

of his part, and accepts it
with panic and protest, but understanding.
Another's need fulfilled.

Born in pain, brought to near perfection
in delicacy and swiftness, his lot
to be selected at random, and stopped.

Later, in the stillness after the completion,
the others will come for the remains,
moderate and methodical—and also necessary—

to occupy and restore the scene.

Belief and Unbelief

Legendary Figures, in Old Age

I saw there a number of elders
in intimate companionship,
their old shapes without shame,

playing with one another
—with all that remained
of the barbed shafts of Love.

And I heard one of them saying
to those around her:
"We cannot renew the Gift

but we can drain it to the last drop."

Lost Cause

And others, grey-featured and slow-moving,
that were condemned to deal only with the symptoms,
endlessly, to the wasting of their eternity,

and never with effect,
                            because they had not
discovered the causes of their complaints.

Ceremony

I am kneeling before the altar
    under the bowl of blood
    with the seed of living light.

I have yielded to an impulse,
    growing in the cold mornings
    as I passed the great blank door,

and walked through the high darkness,
    in among the pious presences
    praying among their candles,

to kneel at the marble rail,
    with my palms placed together
    before the hidden Host.

*

It is accomplished:
    I find that I am considering
    the detail in the cold stone.

Awareness of the body.
    The breath warm on my fingers.
    My knees damp and chill.

*

I will return through the high dark
    among the shadowy believers
    to the orderly interests of the day.

Foetus of Saint Augustine

It is a while since that dusk, among others,
when they lay together in pleasure,

mouthing each other's names
with eyes half closed, and sighs and body liquids:

the little shape is bent under her heart,
as though examining the terms offered,

or examining the carnal basis
for issues of such spiritual complexity,

or as if listening for a breath of wind
that has passed, and might return.

Genesis

The beginning might have been set among that other people,
at the farthest boundary, near the Northern dark.
Where the grass, in their own rugged words, was plenteous enough
to make the herd animals burst... Swamp dwellers, promiscuous,
the users of wicker vessels covered with skins.

Their stories, too, were of exile and dispossession,
family division, fatal women, honour and shame,
rivalry, wrath, alien kings, births foretold or exchanged.
And Fate took shape once and settled among them.
On a great stone, as a bird with black wings.

Prayer I

In a disordered and misguided community
it is the accomplished and the more fulfilled
who are to be found to one side,
unwilling to take part.

Dear God, let the minds and hearts
of the main body heal and fulfil
and we will watch for the first sign
of redemption:

                a turning away
from regard beyond proper merit,
or reward beyond real need,
toward the essence and the source.

Prayer II

That the humours settling
    hard in our heart
may add to the current
    of understanding.

That the rough course
    of the way forward
may keep us alert
    for the while remaining.

Addendum

And remember that My ways
that can seem in the short term
mysterious and unfair
and punishing to the innocent

will justify in the end
the seeker after justice
and not the power seeker
crumpled in his corner.

Belief and Unbelief is number 27 in the Peppercanister series by Thomas Kinsella. It is set in 11.5 Adobe Garamond and published in a paperback edition of 500 copies.

First published June 2007